TODDLER TALK©

The First Signs of Intelligent Life

Joseph Garcia

edited by Dara Burrows

STRATTON
KEHL

PUBLICATIONS, INC. PORT ANGELES, WASHINGTON

P. O. Box 28567
Bellingham, WA
98228 - 0567
1-800-566-6656

An order form is located at the end of the book.

Library of Congress Catalog Card Number 93-84098
ISBN 0-9636229-4-3

Printed with soy ink

To my parents, Emma and Bill Garcia,
who taught me that through learning
and loving, I could do anything.

Cover Design & Photo
    Matt Anderson

Cover Photo
    Emily Brooke Anderson
    (at 8 months signing "think")

Illustrations
    Gregory Maes
    Heather Nystrom
    Lola Roberson

Cartoons
    Matt Anderson

Layout
    Terry Stratton
    Dara Burrows
    Joseph Garcia

I want to give special thanks to Dara Burrows, my wife, for her patience and persistence in transforming my thesis into a readable guide. Thanks also to John Herum for his technical guidance.

I am grateful to all the researchers whose studies confirmed my intuitions about infants' intelligence. And a special acknowledgment goes to Dr. Glenn Massay who encouraged me to investigate my idea, test my theories, and write this book.

This book is bound in a lay-flat cover. Open the book until the back of the spine creases. Do this several times, creasing in a different spot each time. This allows the book to lay flat without breaking the spine.

CONTENTS

COMMUNICATION: THE BACKBONE TO A HEALTHY RELATIONSHIP WITH YOUR CHILD

From the moment babies are born, these tiny human beings start communicating with the world around them. The vital connection between you and your infants depends on this communication. Infants will use extensive body language, facial expressions, and all sorts of verbal sounds to interact with you. These movements and sounds will eventually evolve into language. But until they do, you may have an incredibly difficult time understanding your infants' attempts to tell you things.

How many times have you wished you could look into your babies' minds and know what was going on in there? How many parents have felt the instinctual longing to extract a thought or a word from their troubled infants? The inability to understand your infants is certainly not because you don't try hard enough, or because the infants abandon their attempts to express themselves. Infants have an instinctual need to communicate with you, just as you have an instinctual need to understand them.

Infants are born with abundant intelligence. However, they have a limited means to let you know what their thoughts and needs are. Their undeveloped vocal cords restrict them from participating in the verbal language around them. Imagine how it must feel to be a baby who has many specific needs and thoughts to express, but has no effective way to make those specific needs or thoughts understood. It must be frustrating for these small and socially dependent beings to live with these limitations.

Communication is one of the highest forms of social interaction. Leading researchers in infant behavior have determined that social interaction is crucial to all infants' development. They have further concluded that for a caregiver to withhold social responses to an infant's attempts to communicate is one of the most disruptive things that can occur in the infant's learning process.

What can you do to *encourage* this learning process? Here is where Toddler Talk can contribute to your infants' development. Imagine how your babies might feel if one day you started using simple hand movements to communicate. Let's say you make a particular motion during a certain daily activity, like eating. Soon your infants associate that movement with whatever situation or activity was taking place when the motion was introduced. They begin to experiment with their own hands and discover they can replicate the movements you make. Quickly your babies learn that, by making these motions, they can communicate their needs and wants.

The time between birth and when your infants make their first recognizable words is traditionally lacking in precise communication. This does not have to be the case. These precious months can be rich in meaningful and effective infant/parent interaction. Using manual communication with your infants can help build a solid foundation for mutual understanding. It can also dramatically contribute to the bonding process.

911...To call or not to call?

As a parent, I found that there's nothing more frightening, frustrating, or heartbreaking than when your young toddler comes to you crying and you have no idea what's wrong. I can remember being a toddler and not understanding why the rest of the world didn't know what I was feeling. It never dawned on me that it would take more than crying to let my parents know what was wrong.

The somewhat unusual anecdote which follows illustrates, first of all, that strange and scary things really *can* happen to your toddler. It also shows one extremely practical reason for learning Toddler Talk.

Imagine your toddler Juliet is eleven months old and just learning to walk. She hasn't made her first solo step, but she can really cover some ground balancing herself against the couch. She is doing just that when she plops down onto her bottom, rolls over on her tummy, and happily explores the floor underneath the couch.

She laughs and coos and makes her delightful infant noises. She's been exploring her vocal chords lately, and has come up with some wild sounds. But she hasn't said any clear words yet, other than "mama," "papa," "bye bye" and "uh oh."

Suddenly her bubbling banter turns to a distressed whimper. She sits up and turns to find you. You are sitting nearby wondering what happened. Then Juliet looks at you intently and stops her crying for a moment while she raises her hands and bumps the tips of her index fingers together in front of her nose.

You recognize her hand motion—it means pain. You've been showing her this sign for about three months. After watching you do it, now *she* can make the sign. And, not only does she know what the sign means, but she can *use* it to tell you about her pain.

You pick Juliet up, thinking to yourself, "She made the gesture in front of her nose, so that's where she must hurt." You examine her nose. "Hmmm…it looks okay, but she's still crying. Maybe she bumped her nose on the floor."

Then she looks at you and repeats her hand motion in front of her nose. You wonder, "What can be wrong?" You bend her head back slightly and look a little closer. That's when you see something lodged way up inside her nostril. It's her brother's toy train wheel that broke off his train that morning.

You carefully remove the wheel from Juliet's nose, and soon her crying stops. She looks at you with satisfaction. She was able to tell you what was wrong. You were able to respond. What a relief!

THE BIRTH OF TODDLER TALK

I've always been intrigued by manual language, even though no one in my family is deaf. So, about eighteen years ago, I learned sign language. I enjoyed signing and soon began using it in my work and social life. I was spending time with my deaf friends, some of whom had hearing children. I noticed that hearing children of deaf parents started communicating with sign language at an earlier age than other hearing children did with words.

Intrigued by this observation, I decided to research early childhood language acquisition and the part sign language could play in this process. I was in graduate school at the time, and chose this topic for my thesis. I read about the research that had already been done in pre-speech communication and became especially inspired by the work of Margaret Bullowa, Katherine Nelson, and Timothy Moore. These researchers confirmed that pre-speech infants have the intelligence to communicate specific thoughts and needs.

As I researched further, I found plenty of information on deaf children and their language development. But I couldn't find much information on hearing children using sign language (such as siblings of deaf children using signs). I wondered, what would be the result of using signs for early communication between hearing children and hearing parents. The more I researched, the more I became convinced that I was uncovering a significant treasure.

My next step was to find out *how much* earlier a child could communicate with signs than with words. After consulting with experts in infant development and doing some field research, I concluded that you can begin parent/infant communication at eight months using signs, rather than waiting for comprehensible speech to develop at sixteen to eighteen months.

The births of my two sons in 1985 and '87 gave me perfect opportunities to use and develop Toddler Talk. Looking into my new-born sons' eyes, I could see and feel their innate intelligence and their desire to communicate. It was exciting to be living out, in my day-to-day interactions, the theories and ideas I had been researching. It's hard for me to put into words how wonderful I felt when my sons began to communicate with me at such an early age. Our communication helped me become more in tune, not only with my children, but also with myself as a parent.

Other parents have experienced these rewards, too. The families participating in the studies included parents with no signing experience and some with signing experience. All the parents were surprised at how young their infants were when they started signing. They were also extremely grateful for this tool.

GET THE BIG PICTURE

To get the big picture, please read the entire book before you try anything with your infants. It's important that you understand what's involved in infant communication before you start introducing signs. There's a little bit of background and discussion followed by how-to steps and suggestions. The vocabulary section at the end of the book has drawings and instructions explaining each sign. You can use this section as a workbook and keep track of your child's progress, or write notes and reminders to yourself.

SOMETHING DONE WRONG LONG ENOUGH BECOMES RIGHT?

Believe it or not, less than fifty years ago, many pediatricians in this country told parents that infants were too fragile to be picked up or cuddled. People actually viewed holding and touching infants as something harmful to the infants. And most parents followed this advice. Finally, in the 1940's, a publication refuting this practice went around the country and this attitude began to change. Not until then were parents advised that it was okay to pick up and play with their infants.

Although it may be difficult to imagine that only half a century ago infants were seldom cuddled or caressed, this was the norm. Similarly, for years people have seen manual communication only as a tool for the Deaf. I've encountered people with the attitude that a person who signs is defective or somehow less than normal—whatever "normal" means. Fortunately, we are constantly discovering and adopting more sensible ways to approach new and different things.

Communication, like physical contact, is an essential component in our children's development. We can benefit from the powerful gift the Deaf have given us. That gift is actually a treasure waiting to be unlocked. And the key to that treasure is in your hands.

Why the First Signs of Intelligent Life are Signs

Most people haven't used sign language, so it may be hard to imagine communicating without spoken words. This is why many parents wait until their child can clearly speak before they earnestly begin to focus on two-way communication. However, recent studies indicate that children can absorb and communicate information shortly after birth.

Authorities suggest that 90% of the information we absorb is received through our vision. This means visual acuity is extremely important in our overall development. Infants will naturally use vision to help guide them through the early months of life. Using their vision as a vehicle for communication will give them more opportunities to develop their visual acuity.

Infants naturally use smiling, cooing, and crying to communicate their needs and feelings. They understand a lot about themselves and the world around them. What they lack is a precise way to express their understanding. (Like, "Mommy my stomach hurts" or "I want more food.")

Most infants' vocal cords must develop for sixteen or more months before they can pronounce clear words. And usually, children don't begin speaking in two- and three-word sentences until around their eighteenth to twenty-first month.

However, visual and muscular coordination are in place much earlier than that—long before vocal skills mature. In other words, your infants have the ability to use their hands to make signs before they can use speech to clearly communicate. With Toddler Talk, you will give your infants a way to express themselves which will be more precise and effective than smiling, cooing, and crying. Your young toddlers can use single signs (and many times several signs together) nearly one year before they effectively use speech.

Signs themselves, have certain advantages over words. Signs are often iconic—they represent the shape of objects or they mimic an activity or movement. Therefore, they can be easily recognized and remembered. Words, on the other hand (no pun intended), are more arbitrary and lack an obvious connection to what is being expressed.

Take the sign **eat**, for example. The hand mimics putting something in the mouth. The word "eat" could be said in a number of different languages and sound different in each. But what other gesture, anywhere on the earth, could better show the action of eating?

EAT

"EVEN THOUGH I CAN'T TALK YET, I KNOW MORE THAN YOU THINK I KNOW"

Your infant is born intelligent and has quite a sophisticated idea of what is going on much earlier than many people may think. This intelligence needs to be nurtured by you, the caregiver. The learning process begins moments after birth and quickly accelerates during the first few months of life. Infants are born with a hunger for your contact and communication. They are continuously searching for ways to express themselves. They are looking to you for cues to help them communicate their needs and express their feelings.

Infants can make sense of our complex world long before they can react to it through signs or speech. Your infants understand that communication is going on. They want to be part of that communication much earlier than they are able to tell you. In their desire to express themselves, they will use whatever mode of communication is presented to them.

How your child's cognitive skills and motor coordination develop during infancy

Dr. Eugene Johnson, a child psychologist, has provided the following overview of a typical child's mental and physical development during the first two years of life. He divided infant development into stages—4 months, 8 months, 12 months, etc. These stages are averages based on the many infants observed in research. However, all infants are unique, and will have their own individual timetables.

"Growth during the first two years is more rapid than at any other time in one's life. Research suggests that, by the age of 4 months, infants are capable of remembering sounds and objects, as well as examining parts of their bodies. At 8 months they can play some social games and begin to imitate gestures and actions performed by adults. At this stage they are potentially ready for Toddler Talk interaction. Their motor skills have developed to a point where they are capable of manipulating objects in their hands and standing with support.

By 12 months, infants begin to pretend by symbolically representing familiar activities, such as drinking and eating. They begin to develop choice and will select activities that are desirable. Motor development has continued to improve and further abilities to produce signs have increased. A better understanding of the use of objects and their intended purposes has developed. Advanced motor skills support the development of an increasing number of Toddler Talk signs.

By the end of infancy, at 24 months, cognitive development has improved to a point where children are consistently representing objects with verbal responses and possibly with signs. Motor coordination has developed to a point where more fluid movements are possible, allowing for a larger sign vocabulary."

SEEING THE WORLD THROUGH A NEWCOMER'S EYES

In their first few months of life, everything infants experience is new to them. Infants do not perceive the world as adults would because infants have fewer memories or associations to draw from. Thinking is nothing more than combining and rearranging what is in our memory. The more memories we have, the more raw material there is to produce our thoughts.

Often, infants are experiencing things for the first time that you've seen countless times. These experiences can make a profound impression on an infant's mind. They are the basis for their learning.

Recent conversations I've had with my parents reveal that some things I clearly recall from my early years totally escaped them. Apparently, those things stuck in *my* memory, but were insignificant to my parents. The conclusion is that you never know what event will fix itself in your infant's memory. Be sensitive to your infant's perception. Doing this will help you understand the potential for things which impact your infant's memories.

SHARED PERCEPTION AND SHARED MEANING

You need to be alert to your children's perception; it is *their* perception that will determine the meaning they associate with the signs you show them. Your ability to connect with them on their level of perception will help them learn how to communicate.

Infants will give the meaning you intend to a sign if it is shown to them in the correct situation—at a moment when both of you are experiencing the same thing. They will automatically connect that sign to the shared experience. Therefore, you establish shared meaning between you and your infants through the signs you give to them.

Imagine you are looking at a beautiful sunset and you hold your toddler Joey up to see it too. Then, you show him the sign which means sunset. But his focus is on something closer than yours. He sees a cow in the field between you and the sunset. The meaning you intended for that sign—sunset—is different from the meaning Joey gave it—cow. (Just think, Joey might go through life thinking that a cow is a sunset, and chances are he won't make it through veterinary school.)

LEARNING BY ASSOCIATION

Any person, infant or adult, learns through association. We learn something new by associating it with something familiar to us. However, in their world of basic survival, infants find far fewer important things than we do, and therefore need a smaller array of words or gestures. Their lives are not cluttered with the concerns that, unfortunately, fill most adults' lives. So, just what *is* important to infants?

During the first months of life, the important things will be limited to the essentials: the caregivers' love and touch, food, and the feelings of comfort (such as being warm and being changed). That is why, in most cases, "ma-ma" or "da-da" is the first word to come out of their mouths. You the caregivers are the ones who provide them with the essentials and are your infant's most important "associates" in early life.

If you start making the sound "daddy" enough times when dad walks into the room, before long, your little toddler Emma will associate that new sound with the big guy with a low voice who gives her love, and a bottle, and occasionally (if she's lucky) a clean diaper. Emma will learn Toddler Talk exactly the same way she learns words. For example, when you make the sign **eat** as she starts to eat, that visual symbol will soon be associated in her mind with the mushy stuff that tastes good and is fun to throw.

WILL SIGNING INTERFERE WITH MY CHILD'S SPEECH DEVELOPMENT?

Several parents have wondered whether using Toddler Talk would interfere with normal speech development. This is a natural concern, but you need not worry. Just because infants learn one mode of communication doesn't mean that the first language form will replace or restrict another. As I have said, children have an insatiable intellectual hunger and curiosity, and their ability to absorb new information is immense.

I found nothing in the scientific literature to indicate that this approach to earlier communication will retard learning or verbal development in hearing children. In fact, I found just the opposite; there is considerable research supporting the fact that children exposed to several languages early in life achieve higher levels of language competency later on. In my experience, the children exposed to this early language system have shown above-average understanding of English syntax earlier than those who did not use signs.

The important thing is that using signs to communicate before speech develops will enhance the overall communication process.

The parents in the families using Toddler Talk reported their children began talking around the same age as other children not using Toddler Talk. However, those who had not learned Toddler Talk were just starting to identify objects with words, while our children were already talking *about* those objects. The Toddler Talk children had the advantage of previously learning how to identify objects and feelings through signs.

MORE ADVANTAGES TO USING THE HANDS

Infants are naturally attracted by movement, especially when it's mama, papa, or a caregiver doing the moving. Your infants' visual acuity will be exercised by watching you talk to them with signs. Instead of just glancing at you, they will begin to watch you and focus on your visual communication patterns.

I contend that attempting to use the hands early in life will help infants develop dexterity and muscular control. When these fine motor skills develop and your infants begin to use their hands to communicate, their eye/hand coordination will also improve.

I'd like to further suggest that the brain's right hemisphere is stimulated from using a manual language. The left hemisphere expresses thoughts in words and translates words into thoughts. It uses a step by step process to break down thoughts into parts which can be systematically organized and understood. The right hemisphere processes non-verbal sensory images and can recognize and manipulate visual patterns. It can see something conceptually as a whole without methodically dissecting it in order to understand. The right hemisphere influences personality, insight, imagination, and initiative.

So, when a baby is exposed to words, the brain's left hemisphere is stimulated. By adding visual language you also stimulate the right hemisphere which often doesn't get as much nurturing. Developing and using all the resources available allows people to realize their full potential.

Watching you talk with your hands will help satisfy your infant's need for complete mental stimulation. Toddler Talk may not necessarily make your child more intelligent. However, scientific literature is full of research supporting the fact that lots of parent/child interaction contributes to the child's full and healthy mental and emotional development.

To CONTRIBUTE OR TO COMMIT?

A pig and a hen were walking together in the barnyard. The hen said, "Our farmer has been so good to us. We should somehow repay him for his kindness." "What do you have in mind?" asked the pig. "Well," suggested the hen, "how about serving him a fine ham and egg breakfast?" The pig thought for a moment then replied, "For you that's a contribution—for me it's a commitment!"

Learning Toddler Talk will require only a small contribution of your time. Reactions to things you and your children see, things you do, and things your children do, will now be expressed through your hands, face, and body, as well as through your voice.

THE HOW TO'S OF TODDLER TALK

LET YOUR FINGERS DO THE TALKING

Later in the book I will explain the first signs infants respond to quickly. Start getting familiar with those signs you will be introducing first. Try using them with other family members or friends during every-day activities. Let learning the signs be enjoyable. The last thing you want is for Toddler Talk to be a burden or a chore.

With a little practice you can become spontaneous and natural with your signs. Some focused time with your infants will help you identify the various signals they send that let you know they are ready to start. By the time your children's gazes start connecting with yours, you will be ready to introduce signs.

GAZES: OPPORTUNE MOMENTS FOR INITIATING SIGNS

As you focus on your infant's behavior and habits, you will recognize different kinds of gazes happening between you. These gazes are instances of mutual perception and are the moments to introduce signs. Try to anticipate when these gazes are about to occur, and be ready to respond with a sign. Three kinds of gazes provide good opportunities to introduce signs.

Expressive gazes happen when your infant has a need, or wants to express a feeling, or ask a question.

Suppose your infant Danielle is eating some applesauce and she finishes it before she has had enough. She looks to you for more. That instant you make eye contact with her, her eyes are saying "more." This is what I call an *expressive gaze*. This would be a perfect time to introduce the sign **more?**

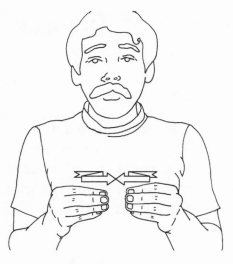

MORE

Chance mutual gazes happen when you and your infant look at each other at the same time by chance, or for no particular reason.

Imagine you are sitting across from your infant son, Raymond. His eyes scan the room until they meets yours. For a moment, you are connected by your gaze. Your child's attention is completely on you for that instant. This is a *chance mutual gaze*. At this moment, your son is receptive to whatever you communicate to him. This is a good time to introduce a sign for something in the room, like a book that you are about to read to him.

Pointed gazes happen when you and your child look at the same thing at the same time and then look at each other.

A cat walks in the room and meows. You and your daughter Nicole both look at the cat and then at each other. The instant Nicole returns her gaze to you, you make the **cat** sign and point to the cat. *Pointed gaze* episodes will happen more and more as your children are shown more signs for the things they see and experience.

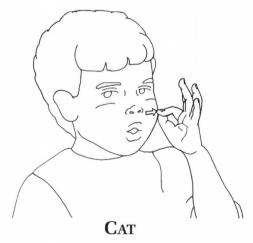

CAT

LET'S FACE IT

During infancy, your child takes in an incredible amount of information from your facial expressions. Vivid expressions will help give your signs and words more meaning.

Adding the appropriate expression will also enhance your child's understanding of whatever you are communicating. In some cases, the face carries as much meaning as the sign or word itself. Use your face generously.

Notice in the pictures below, the sign for **little** shows the shoulders hunched and the eyes squinting. Also notice the expressions when signing **cold** and **pain.** Every utterance has the potential to carry an expression.

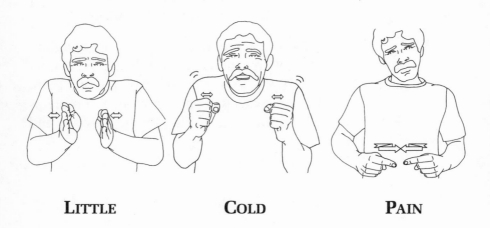

LITTLE   COLD   PAIN

THE FIRST SIGN OF INTELLIGENT LIFE

My son Stratton was eight months old when he made his first sign. I had been showing him the sign **more** for the last two months whenever I suspected he might have been wanting more of something. On this particular evening, he was in his high chair eating dinner. He ate a few peas and then accidentally knocked the rest on the floor. He looked up at me and signed **more.** He made the sign as if he had been using it for a long time. He seemed to know I would understand and respond to his request.

I tried to be cool and calm, but inside I was jumping up and down. I wanted to find a balance between teaching him to be careful with his food and showing my joy that he signed his first word. Anyway, I quickly brought him some more peas. My smile took a while to go away. After that, he used the **more** sign in many appropriate situations.

By the way, I usually voiced the word "more" at the same time I signed **more.** I noticed that on occasion Stratton would vocalize a sound while he made the sign. The sound evolved from a grunt to a "ma" sound over several months. Other parents experienced similar responses from their infants.

How to Show Your Infant a Sign

The best time to introduce a sign varies according to the situation. Sometimes just *before* you do something is best. Other times showing a sign *during* an experience works well, and occasionally, showing a sign immediately *after* an occurrence will help make the association most clear. The best times to show some of the first few basic signs are explained in the sections that follow.

For other signs that are not explained in the next few sections, you will get a feel for the best approach to use by interacting with your infants. Your children will eventually connect the experience to the sign. Shared meaning will be established between you and your children following several repeated episodes. After your infants' first attempts to make the sign are rewarded with the response they wanted, they will be motivated to learn more. Your children will hunger for signs to satisfy their ever-increasing needs, desires, and curiosities.

I recommend you sign close to your eyes the instant your child looks at you. It's important to make the sign close to your face directly in the sight-line between you and your child.

After showing a sign for several weeks, I found it helpful to shape and move my infant's hands immediately after I made the sign. Eventually, my son would offer me his hands, wanting me to move them for him. I always made this process into a game and didn't *expect* any solo signing by him. After all, this isn't a drill, just loving play that helps him link the movements with communication. One parent remarked that it was too bad we couldn't reach into our babies' mouths (doing the same thing we can with their hands) and shape their tongues and teeth.

Repeat the sign every time you show it. Reward your children's attempts to make a sign. Show your enthusiasm and repeat the sign again. I usually throw in a hug. I like hugs.

WHICH SIGNS TO START WITH AND WHEN TO START

Child psychologists have learned that toddlers understand the following six basic concepts and can use them early in their communication. The following list will help you identify the concepts your children will understand and the types of things your infants may want to learn signs for.

1. what something is (milk, a dog, a book)

2. addressing someone (papa, mama, grandma)

3. where something is (where shoe?, where cat?)

4. something gone (no toy, food all gone)

5. recurrence (more milk, hide again)

6. possession (my bear, your sock)

Initially, every-day simple activities and needs such as eating, drinking milk, changing diapers, or wanting more of something are perfect opportunities to introduce signs. I suggest you start with the signs **milk, more,** and **eat**, which are among the simplest to make. Keep making these signs for at least a month before adding other signs. Don't overload your infant at the beginning. Stick to these basic signs until your infant starts making them. Then continue the first few and gradually add more.

Most families participating in Toddler Talk research started showing their infants signs around their children's sixth or seventh month. We also had families start with older toddlers, around eight to eleven months. You can start showing your infants signs as early or as late as you wish, but generally, not until around their sixth month can they focus enough to retain a sign's image for future reference.

EAT

As you are about to feed your babies, you sign **eat.** Show your infants the sign before each feeding time and while you are feeding them or while they are attempting to feed themselves. Eventually, as your infants learn what the sign means, they will use it when they want to eat. Several parents mentioned they were able to tell if their infants were hungry or not, simply by making the sign and watching their infants' reactions.

Eᴀᴛ

One family was using Toddler Talk with their nine-month old daughter. The parents had been showing her signs for three months, but she hadn't signed anything yet. One day the mother said to her child, without using any signs: "Go tell daddy it's time to eat." The little nine-month-old rolled her walker over to her father, looked at him and made the **eat** sign. This was her first sign. It's interesting how sometimes a child will decide to start signing or talking all of a sudden.

Mᴏʀᴇ?

If the bottle or breast empties, or your infants run out of food, or simply stop eating, sign **more?** (with an inquisitive facial expression). Then allow a very slight pause, before giving them more. Children sometimes associate this sign with hunger and are likely to make the **more** sign when they are hungry. As their understanding becomes more sophisticated, they will differentiate between **more?** and **eat**. In several families, **more** was the first sign their infants produced.

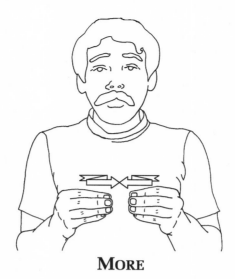

MORE

Shortly after my first son (at eight months) learned the sign **more**, he used it frequently. Often when we were playing a tickle or a make-a-funny-face game, and I would stop playing, he would sign **more, more**.

MILK

Every time your infants drink milk (whether from the breast or bottle) you show the **milk** sign, immediately before and after they drink.

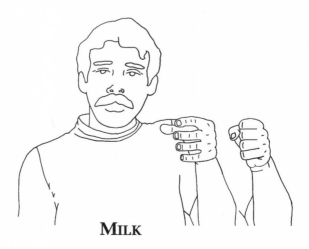

MILK

Once your infants request milk (by making the milk sign) and are rewarded, they will understand that their motion brings results (milk). Sometimes infants use this sign to mean anything to drink. Be aware of this and eventually offer other signs for other liquids.

Many infants make the **milk** and **more** signs during their eighth month if these signs are introduced during their sixth month and repeated often during appropriate situations.

TOILET

Another sign to introduce early is **toilet**. Show this sign when you know your infants are urinating or defecating. After some time, your children are likely to make this sign when they are wetting their diaper or moving their bowels. Eventually, they will learn to sign **toilet** just before or while they relieve themselves.

TOILET

We found that parents used this sign more than infants did. While the infants understood the sign, they didn't initiate it very often. I believe the reason may have something to do with the newer diapers that draw the wetness away from babies' skin.

These diapers are more tolerable when wet than cloth diapers. So, babies who wear new fiber diapers may find the changing experience less desirable than wearing wet diapers that don't feel wet. Those parents using cloth diapers may see their children make this sign more often, as they want the comfort of a nice dry diaper. (By the way, this is not a plug for disposable diapers.)

Showing the **toilet** sign early can be useful in later toilet training. Your children will have a quick and easy way to tell you they have to go. This sign can also eliminate unnecessary embarrassment for an older child who has to go or who has already had an accident, but doesn't want anyone but a parent to know about it. I use this sign even now with my sons who are six and eight. At times, the boys are so excited and so involved in their activities that they ignore nature's call. I notice their little dance and subtly motion **toilet** to them. That brings them back to the reality that they are not Superman, and need a few moments to take care of business.

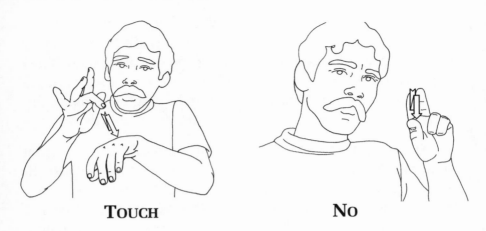

TOUCH   NO

TOUCH-NO

Suppose you and your child Aaron are visiting a friend whose house is filled with plants. Aaron toddles about, exploring the greenery. While you are talking with your friend, Aaron discovers a plant that looks different from the others. He is extra curious about this unusual green thing, and so he touches it. As it turns out, this strange green thing is a cactus. You sign **touch-no** as you comfort Aaron and remove the cactus needles from his fingers.

It may not be a cactus, but at some time your infants will reach for something that could hurt them. The important thing is that the moment when your infants touch or are about to touch something that will cause them harm is the time to introduce the **touch-no** sign. Unfortunately, sometimes infants have to learn the hard way. Your infants will connect the sign **touch-no** with whatever discomfort they experience from their environment. This will allow you to use **touch-no** as a warning and prevent other injuries.

Here is an imaginary situation which demonstrates another advantage to using **touch-no**. Let's say you and your toddler Amber, who is fourteen months old, are visiting a friend who has a dog.

Like many children, Amber is especially fond of trying to pull out the hair on every furry little animal she sees. You say to her in words, "Don't bother the dog over there." Amber sees you pointing at the dog. The only word in your sentence she understands may be "dog." In her excitement of recognizing the word "dog," she may very well run up to the dog and point at its face (or try to pluck the little fella hairless) to show you she understands "dog"—which, of course, is exactly what you were trying to avoid.

This kind of miscommunication can be prevented by understanding how your child learns language. Then you can adjust your communication to fit her way of perceiving the world. It is better to simply identify the object and give a command than it is to supply her with a complex sentence containing only one or two words she can relate a meaning to. If she had already understood the sign **touch-no**, it would have been more effective to sign **dog, touch-no** as you say to her, "Don't touch the dog."

Those parents who introduced the **touch-no** sign early in their children's lives are glad they did; their toddlers understood and followed this warning.

Usually children don't produce **touch-no**—it's a caregiver's command. Some children did produce the **touch** sign and then look to their parents for approval. Several parents told me they saw their toddlers sign **touch-no** to other children, warning them of danger.

HOT, WARM, AND COLD

Hot and **cold** are useful signs and can be introduced during feeding time. For example, you have a dish of food that is too hot to eat. The steam is still rising as you set it on the table out of reach of your toddler. You point to the food and sign **hot.** The steam coming from food gives your child something visual to associate with hot.

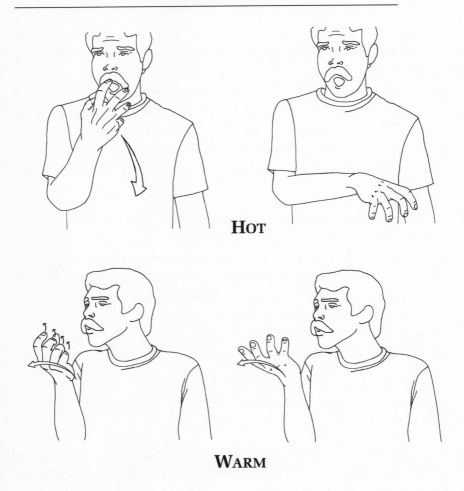

HOT

WARM

A warm bowl of water next to a cool bowl of water is a good way to introduce **warm** and **cold**. Experiment with each bowl, allowing your children to feel the water, then show them the appropriate sign.

COLD

"CAN YOU TELL ME WHERE IT HURTS?"

Toddler Talk offers this unique benefit: it provides a way for your children to tell you where they are hurt. When they come to you crying, show them the **pain** sign as you console them. Make the sign at the injured area. After a short time, your infants will associate pain with this sign. Once they learn this relationship between an injury and the **pain** sign, the stage is set for locating their pain.

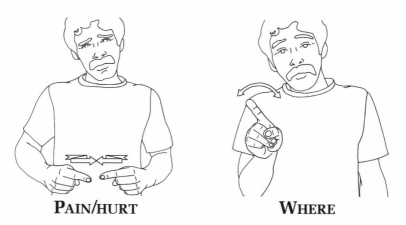

PAIN/HURT   **WHERE**

It's interesting that when asked **where pain?**, many children point to the *object* that hurt them rather than showing *where* they are hurt on their bodies.

Here's what to try when your children are hurt and you have no idea what happened or where they are hurt. You sign **pain,** and then **where?** Then sign **search** as you move the **search** sign around their bodies. I found it helpful to sign **pain-where?** then touch my son's head, and sign **pain** there? (pointing to a spot). I would go over his whole body in this way until he nodded his head, yes. This process was successful in locating the injury with many children.

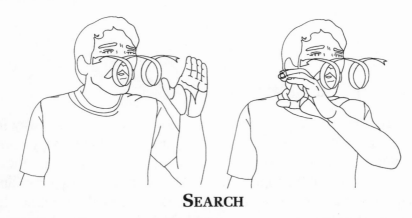

SEARCH

After a few episodes of searching for the pain, your child will get the message and direct you to the injured area without going through the entire search process.

Kim was 14 months, and playing in the park, when she stumbled and fell. Her mother jumped up from her bench, looked at Kim and signed **hurt?** Kim shook her head "no" and went on playing. Later, when they had returned home, Kim was playing with her rag doll. She fell again, this time landing on her doll. She picked up the doll and went over to her mother. Kim looked sad, so her mother asked if she was hurt, by signing **hurt?** Kim set her doll down and signed **hurt** over the doll. Her mother got a bandage and put it on the doll. Kim picked up her doll and walked away happy.

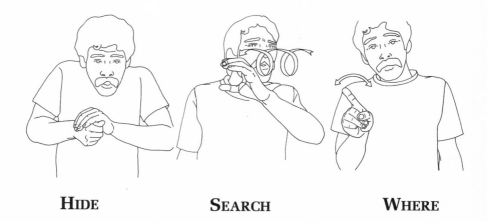

HIDE   **SEARCH**   **WHERE**

SOME HANDY GAMES

Be creative and spontaneous with Toddler Talk. Many signs can be used while playing games. **Hide, search, catch,** and **tickle** are some obvious ones. With three or more people, play hide and seek using the signs **hide, search, where,** and **tickle**. One person hides and the other person goes with the toddler and signs **where** and **search** while looking for the hidden person. When you find the hidden person, you tickle them. This is a good time to show the **catch** sign.

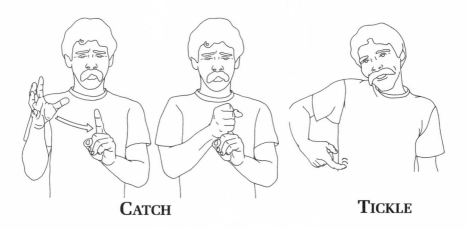

CATCH   **TICKLE**

Older toddlers, about 14 to 18 months, will love this game. While they are looking at you, put a toy or something special to them out of sight, but within a few crawls or steps. Sign **where?** with an inquisitive look on your face. Your toddlers look for the object and when they find it, you give them a hug. Repeat the game, finding a different hiding place each time.

One family invented a game they called "catch the worm." The mother cut off the index finger of an old glove and attached little eyes and a fuzzy pipe cleaner she bought at a craft shop to make it look like a worm or caterpillar. Wearing the worm on her index finger, she would sign **worm** to her daughter.

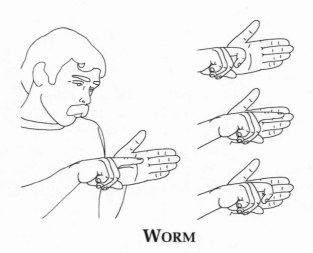

WORM

As her finger moved across the front of her hand, her infant would try to catch the worm. Each time the child caught the worm, the worm would interact with her and she would get a hug. This is one example of the limitless games you can create with signs and your imagination.

I read lots of animal books with pictures to my sons and would make the signs for the animals as we came to them. Eventually this evolved into a game. As we saw the picture, I would say the name, make the animal's sound, and then sign its name. This became very useful when we went to the zoo. I would sign the individual animals as we watched them. My sons would also make the sign for the animals and imitate the sounds I made.

The vocabulary section includes the signs for alligator, bear, bee, bird, bull, butterfly, cat, dog, cow, fish, elephant, frog, fly, horse, lion, insect, monkey, mosquito, mouse, rabbit, snake, squirrel, spider, turtle, and worm. (Let me know what sound you come up with for a worm.)

RECOGNIZING YOUR CHILDREN'S SIGNS

Children may not always make a sign exactly as you make it. Motor skills develop at different rates. Therefore, dexterity levels will vary among children the same age. Notice the difference between the way these children make the **where** sign. The first child points both index fingers and makes the motion with one hand, using the other as a support. The older child signs **where** the regular way except his motion is wider.

WHERE-EARLIER VERSION   **WHERE-LATER VERSION**

Remember, although your children will try their best to imitate your movements, their hand shapes will be crude at first. Keep making the signs correctly, despite your children's variations. They need to see the signs repeated the right way, just as they need to hear words pronounced correctly to perfect their speech.

As I've mentioned, it was helpful to shape my children's hands for some signs. This was especially true when my sons wanted to duplicate the exact finger shape but initially had a difficult time recreating the shape. They would hold up their hands so I could help them form the *specific finger shapes*. This was different from several months earlier when they would offer me their hands to make the sign *movement*. As they got a little older, they wanted to be more exact in replicating my hand shapes.

Here is another example of variations in the way children may form a sign. The first picture shows the way a child at ten months signed **water** by holding up only his index finger. The second picture shows the way the same child at thirteen months made the sign correctly—holding up all three fingers.

WATER-EARLY VERSION   **WATER-LATER VERSION**

My sons were learning Toddler Talk in rural Alaska, where many small planes were flying overhead. So **airplane** was a sign we learned early.

AIRPLANE

When an airplane passed over us, I would look up and point at it. I would sign **airplane** and move my hand in the same direction as the plane. I also made a "rrrrmmmm" sound. Then, I said the word "airplane." At ten and a half months, Stratton used his pointed index finger and moved it over his head making a "rrrrmmmm" sound. Damian, at eleven months, used his fist with the same movement and said "appp."

I remember both children referred to the airplane by making the sign and sound several times later in the day they each had seen it. They were reaffirming their understanding that the sign represented the airplane. This also indicated that the children were thinking about the plane and wanted to talk about it. I realized that they wanted to initiate conversation. Learning the sign **airplane** gave them an opportunity to do this. This was the first time they were able to start a conversation based on an experience we had shared. I reinforced their attempts to discuss the airplane by making the sign and telling them about the airplane—it was loud, it flew high over the trees, and then it disappeared in the distance.

A mother who started Toddler Talk by using the **more** sign told me her six month infant clapped her hands when she wanted something. This child's clapping—a sort of babbling in signs—eventually became **more** as her fingers were able to form the exact shape.

Your child's signs will go through a metamorphosis, sometimes changing over days or weeks. The vocabulary section has enough space so that as you identify the sign variations, you can keep track of your child's progress.

REPEATING AND REINFORCING YOUR SIGNS

Have fun with your whole family using your signs at every possible opportunity. It's advantageous to use signs among all family members so your toddlers see manual communication in their surroundings. Your children are making a connection between the sign and what it represents. This connection is reinforced every time they see or make the sign. Show caregivers such as babysitters the signs your infants use. It may be frustrating to your children if the people who care for them don't understand the signs your children make.

I found that some children respond quickly to some signs and more slowly to others. The age at which each child produces a sign is completely individual. Be patient and consistent. Never stop providing a sign just because you think they know it (you've seen them sign it a few times) or because they don't sign it at all. Keep using the signs. Whatever happens, don't show frustration. This is supposed to be fun for you and your toddlers. If you let them feel that you are disappointed or impatient, they will lose interest and the fun could end.

Set up situations that offer the opportunity to use a sign. During meal times, give your children half as much food as usual and then sign **more?** when they finish the first portion.

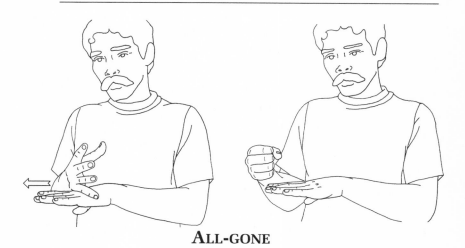

ALL-GONE

Also, when your toddlers finish something on their plates, you can sign **all-gone**. By the way, this sign will soon become handy when you don't want them to have more of something.

Always be prepared to acknowledge your child's attempts to produce signs. Don't wait until your child produces one sign before you introduce another. Use your daily experiences to direct you in the vocabulary you generate.

One thing that really surprised me was that my children would remember and produce signs after not seeing or using them for weeks. My son Stratton was fifteen months old and for several days we kept meeting people with infants.

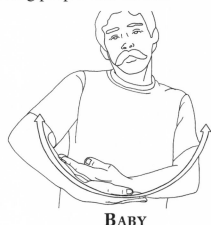

BABY

I showed Stratton the sign for **baby** each time. He never made the sign himself until three weeks later when we saw another baby. He looked at the baby, then made the **baby** sign to me.

Other parents were also amazed at their children's retention. However, do not make the mistake of relying entirely on your child's memory (phenomenal as it may be). You should repeat your signs at every opportunity.

Anticipate your child's needs and use signs throughout your day. Make it a pleasant experience for both of you. Add new signs when the proper situation arises.

COMBINING SIGNS

After your children have made a sign several times, you can begin adding a new sign or one they already know to the first sign: **more-milk; food-all gone; papa-dance; cold-water; where-shoes,** etc.

Touch-no and **hurt** go well together. Many children respond quickly to this combination.

Children will sometimes sign **where-mother** or **father** if either parent is not in sight. **Where** can be used before many objects or people.

HOW TO CREATE A NEW SIGN

Occasionally, something will make an impression on your child and you will want a sign for it but will not find it in the vocabulary section. When this happens you can invent a sign. Make your sign so it mimics an action or shows an object's shape. Be spontaneous when inventing a sign. Create a sign which visually represents the object or situation. Try to recreate the most dramatic characteristic with your hands.

For example, playing an instrument can be imitated once your child sees it being played. Keep the movement simple. Add a facial expression to your sign when it's appropriate.

I suggest you create a sign for each person (or pet) who has regular contact with your child, or for a person whose photograph your child sees regularly. I try to come up with a motion that shows an obvious characteristic of the person (or animal).

Record the new signs you invent and describe their origins. There is space for notes under each term in the vocabulary section. Enter your own signs in the book alphabetically. This will help you and others locate them later. Remember, your child will get confused if you change the way you make a sign from day to day.

All the signs in this book are American Sign Language (ASL) signs. If you prefer to use ASL signs for words not included in this book, you may wish to locate a regular ASL vocabulary book.

THE POWER OF SILENCE

It's natural to want to say the corresponding words with your signs. Vocalizing is almost automatic and you may be tempted to do it all the time. However, remember you are trying to develop your child's visual and analytic senses. A balance between verbal communication and silent eye-to-eye communication is important. I suggest you maintain some silent interaction. Your children's senses are stimulated in different ways by being silent. They draw on other resources and develop different skills when their oral/aural channels take a rest.

THINGS TO REMEMBER

•It's never too late to begin using Toddler Talk. You can even use signs after your toddler begins speaking. It will enhance your communication and add an element of fun to your lives.

•Parents have started using signs as early as the sixth month or as late as a year and a half.

•Get familiar with the first few signs you will use. Many parents have had great success with the signs **more**, **milk**, and **eat** as their first signs.

•Show your infant the signs at every opportunity and be consistent in the way you make your signs.

•After you use the first few signs for a couple of months, introduce more signs, such as the signs for things that interest your infant (a pet, a person) or an object your infant sees often (their shoes, a teddy bear or a book).

•Make your signs in the sight-line, and be ready to use a sign during *chance mutual gazes*, *expressive gazes*, and *pointed gazes*.

•Begin playing signing games like catch, hide, and tickle with your infants.

•When your infants attempt their first signs, encourage them and help them shape their hands.

•Learn more signs and be ready to introduce them at any opportunity or create opportunities to show new signs.

•Always repeat each sign you show. In general, the more your infants see a sign, the faster they will learn it and use it.

•Be patient. Never show disappointment or frustration if your child does not produce a sign. All children are different and need to be treated according to their own timetables and behaviors.

•Have fun. Don't worry, be happy.

THE TERRIBLE TWO'S AND THREE'S, *TALK* YOUR KID OUT OF THEM

Where do the "terrible two's and three's" come from, anyway? Who invented them? Why? How could those little angels turn into such testing bundles of mischief? What is the easiest way to navigate through these years?

Maybe two-or three-year-olds are feeling frustrated because they have just spent their entire lives unable to communicate what they understood or needed. They may have been thinking "I know what's going on, but why don't *you* know that I know?" So, when toddlers *do* gain verbal power, maybe they need to release—it's pay-back time. I suspect the "terrible two's and three's" are partially a result of this communicative frustration.

Remember the imaginary scenario of your toddler Juliet and her hurt nose? Had you not been able to exchange your signs, you both would have felt frustrated. It could have been a terrible experience for you because you wanted so much to understand and help her. It would have been equally frustrating for Juliet because she had something to express and no way to express it.

FINAL THOUGHTS FROM THE AUTHOR

Young children have little or no control over their lives. Communication is one thing that begins to empower them. You the caregivers are the most important influences in your toddlers' world. Communication with you at an early age will feed them emotionally and intellectually. More and more research confirms what wise parents have always known—you will establish the lasting foundation of your child's physical, mental, and spiritual health by meeting all these needs during those first few years. And naturally, the time you share with your child will have more quality when you are more interactive.

My own children are in school now and signing continues to enrich our interaction. With non-verbal communication, our eyes tend to look a little deeper to understand each other. This process leads to a closer sense of connection. I feel that by experiencing communication in this way, you tap a little deeper into the roots of parent/child bonding—the more dynamic your communication the stronger your bond.

As a parent, the Toddler Talk system gave me an incredible satisfaction. I hope you enjoy Toddler Talk and benefit from it as I and others have. Those using this system have all expressed the delight they experienced communicating with their children so early in their children's lives. Many parenting rewards are built on a foundation of good communication.

As long as I've got your attention, I'm going to offer one last suggestion. When your children begin to speak, they will learn and use whatever words you give them. Don't underestimate their intelligence and memory. Use correct and accurate words. Even if they cannot pronounce a word perfectly, they have heard it and will eventually use it in the correct context.

I taught my sons the specific words for injuries (bruise, cut, scrape, etc.). They learned to distinguish the different types of injuries while I noticed other children their ages still said "ouch" or "owie" for all injuries. This is just an example; you can carry this idea through all vocabulary development. Teaching your children a "baby" word for something, only to replace it later with a more sophisticated word, may be doing them a disservice.

I hope you and your family have fun with Toddler Talk. I am interested in hearing about your experiences. Write to me c/o Stratton-Kehl Publications, Inc. Post Office Box 100, Port Angeles, WA 98362.

HAND SHAPES

These hand shapes are borrowed from American Sign Language and are used to explain the signs in the vocabulary section.

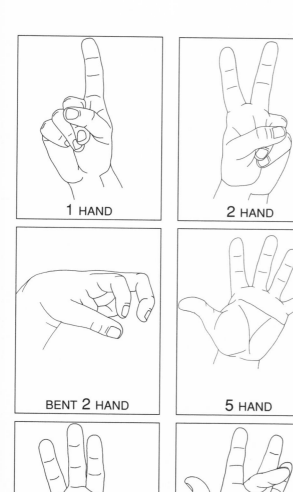

1 HAND

2 HAND

INVERTED 2 HAND

BENT 2 HAND

5 HAND

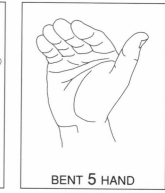

BENT 5 HAND

6 HAND

MODIFIED 8 HAND

9 HAND

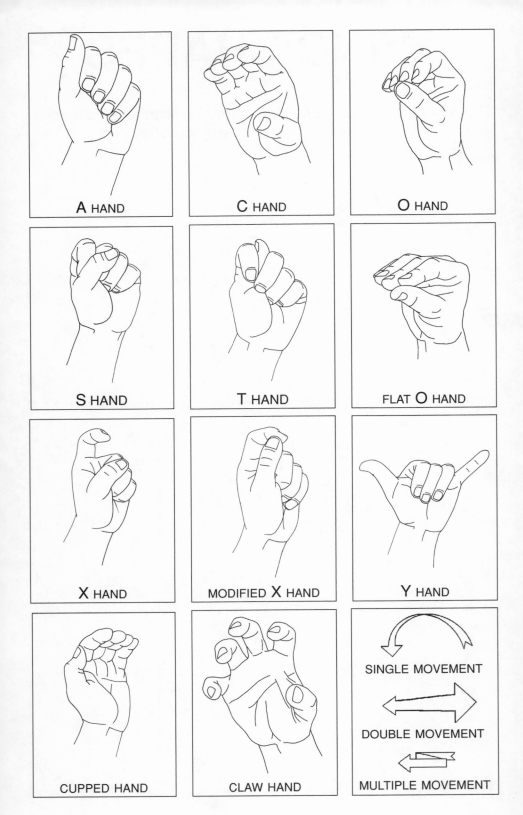

A HAND

C HAND

O HAND

S HAND

T HAND

FLAT O HAND

X HAND

MODIFIED X HAND

Y HAND

CUPPED HAND

CLAW HAND

SINGLE MOVEMENT

DOUBLE MOVEMENT

MULTIPLE MOVEMENT

AGAIN

The cupped action hand arcs down and the fingertips touch the palm of the flat base hand.

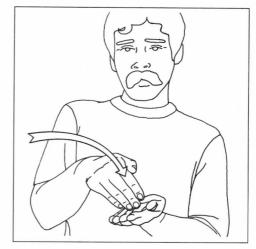

AIRPLANE

The "Y" hand, with the index finger extended and palm down, moves through space to show the flight of an airplane.

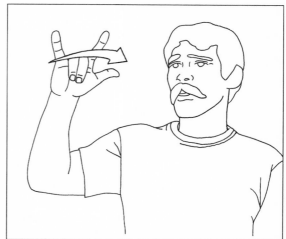

ALL GONE

The flat base hand is held face down. The "5" hand rests on top then slides down the fingers of the base hand and closes into an "S" hand.

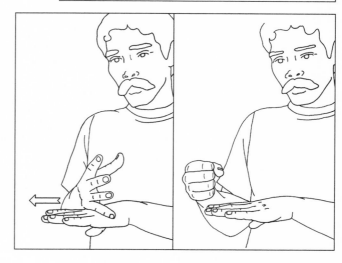

ALLIGATOR

Top and bottom claw hands touch at the wrists. Then the palms touch and the fingers interlace. This motion is repeated, like an alligator's jaw opening and closing.

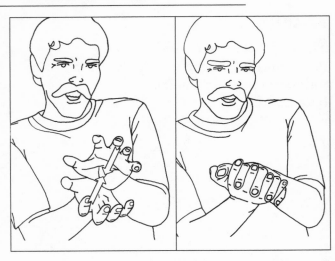

APPLE

The index finger of the "X" hand touches the cheek while the hand twists.

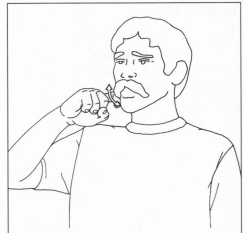

BABY

One arm cradles the other and both move from side to side, as if rocking a baby.

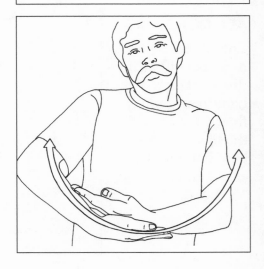

BANANA

The base hand is in the "1" position. The modified "X" hand slides down the side of the "1" index finger several times, as if peeling a banana.

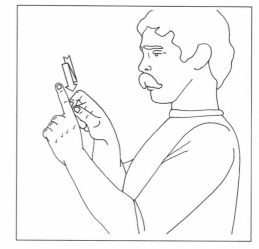

BATH

Both "A" hands rub against the body in circular motions, as though washing the body.

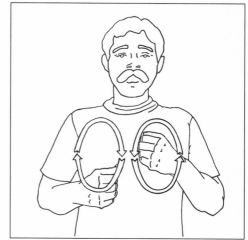

BEAR

Two claw hands are crossed in front of the chest, facing inwards, and make a clawing movement.

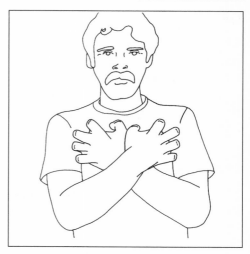

BEAUTIFUL

A "5" hand begins on one side of the face, and circles around the face, closing to a flat "O" hand at the chin.

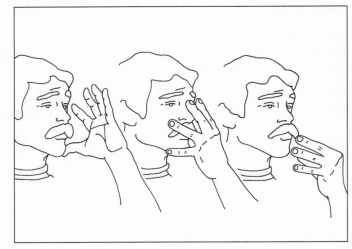

BED

The tilted head is placed on two flat palms held together at the cheek, as if the head were lying on a pillow.

BEE

The "9" action hand touches the corner of the upper lip. Then the same hand takes a "B" position and brushes across the mouth, as if brushing away a bee.

BIG

Both hands, in a bent "L" shape, start in front of the chest and move out to the sides.

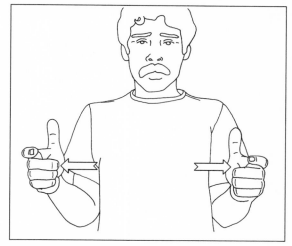

BIRD

The index finger and thumb are held together at the lips. They snap open and closed, like a bird's beak.

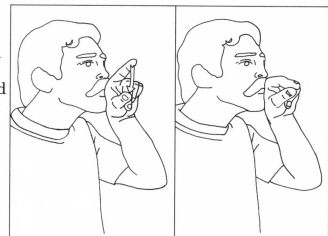

BOOK

Two flat hands are held together, and then open.

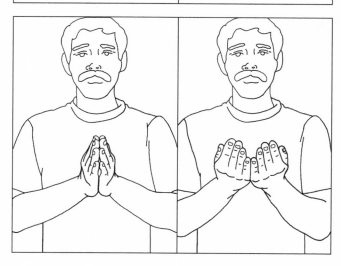

BOTTLE

The flat base hand is held palm up. The "C" action hand taps the base hand several times.

BOY

The hand closes to a flat "O" at forehead, as if grabbing a baseball cap.

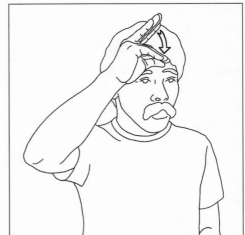

BREAD

The base hand is held palm facing body and the open cupped action hand brushes up and down on the back of the base hand several times.

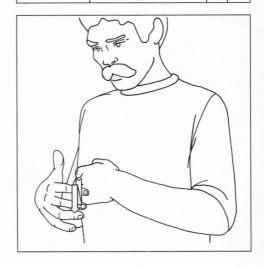

BROTHER

The "L" action hand is held to the forehead, then brought down to the "L" base hand.

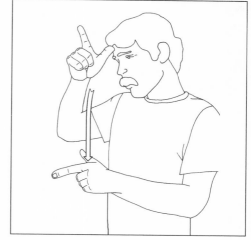

BULL

The index fingers of the "S" hands extend forward at the temples, representing a bull's horns.

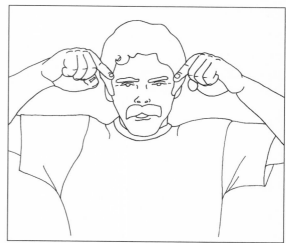

BURN

The base hand is held palm down at chest level. The "5" action hand is held beneath the base hand, with the fingers wiggling to represent flames.

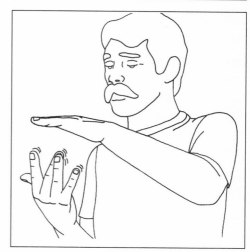

BUTTER

The base hand is held palm
up and the first two fingers
brush the palm, as if spread-
ing butter.

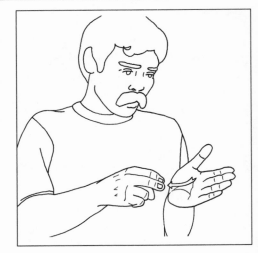

BUTTERFLY

With the palms facing down,
the thumbs lock together and
the hands flap up and down,
like butterfly wings.

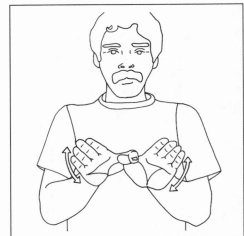

CAKE

The "5" base hand is palm
up. The claw action hand
touches the base palm and
moves up slowly several
inches, like a cake rising.

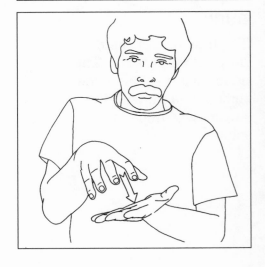

CAR

Both "S" hands are held out at chest level, moving in opposite arc motions, as if steering a car.

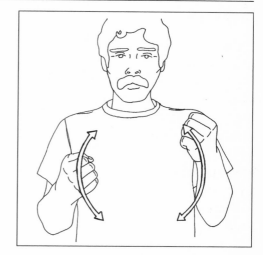

CAT

The "9" hand touches the corner of the upper lip, brushing out and away from the face several times, representing a cat's whiskers.

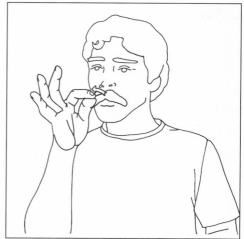

CATCH

The open "5" action hand swoops down and catches the "1" base hand index finger.

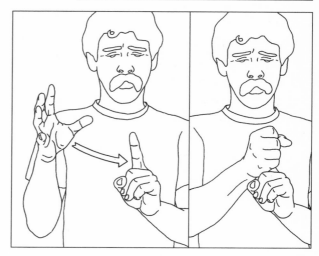

CHANGE

Two "A" hands are held at chest level with the knuckles of one hand resting on side of the thumb of the other hand. Both hands pivot in opposite directions to switch places.

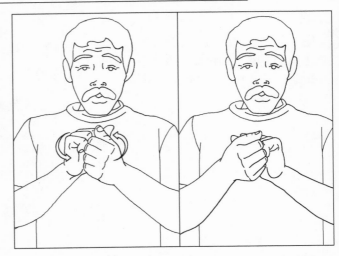

CLEAN

The base hand is held flat with palm facing up. The "A" action hand rubs against the base palm in a circular motion, as if scrubbing or cleaning.

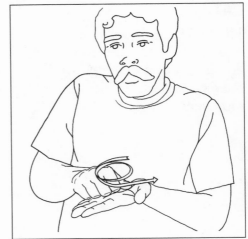

CLOUDS

Both "5" hands are held at eye level, with the palms facing out. The palms turn inwards together with small circular motions, as if the hands were outlining clouds.

COAT

Both "A" hands are held at shoulder level then come together in front of the chest, as if closing a coat.

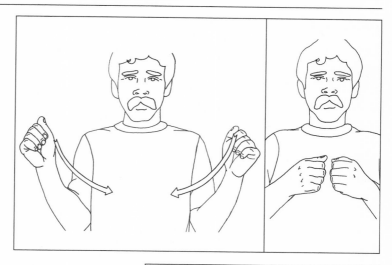

COLD

Both "S" hands are held close to the body at shoulder level with the shoulders hunched and the arms shaking.

COOKIE

The base "5" hand is held palm up. The claw action hand twists around and back again against the palm, making the shape of a cookie.

CORN-ON-THE-COB

Both claw hands are held in front of the mouth, palms facing each other. The hands pivot back and forth, as if turning a cob of corn.

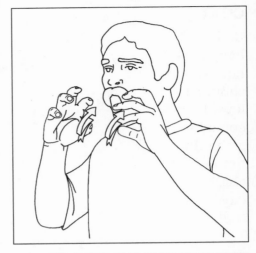

COW

The thumb of the "Y" hand taps the temple several times.

CRY

The index fingers of both "1" hands slide down the cheeks, showing the paths of tears.

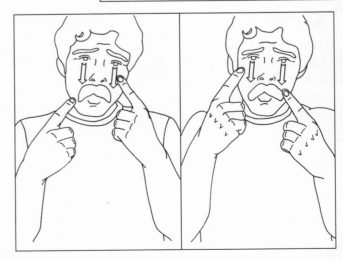

DANCE

The "5" base hand is held with the palm facing up. The inverted "2" hand swings back and forth over the base hand, as if dancing.

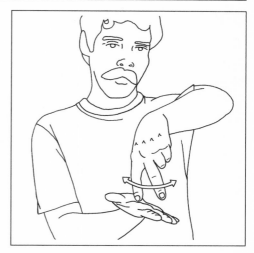

DELICIOUS

The "8" hand is held with the middle finger touching the lips, and the hand pivots out and away from face.

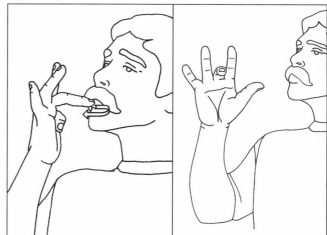

DIRTY

The back of the "5" hand is held under the chin with the fingers wiggling.

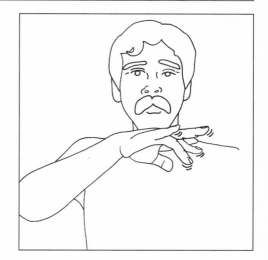

DOG

The middle finger snaps against the thumb, as if calling a dog.

DOWN

The index finger points downward several times.

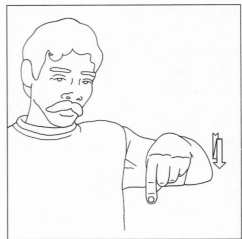

DREAM

The index finger of the "1" hand touches the side of the head, then bends and straightens as it moves away from the head.

DRINK

The "C" hand is held with the thumb at the lower lip, pivoting up.

EARACHE

Both "1" hands tap together several times in front of the ear.

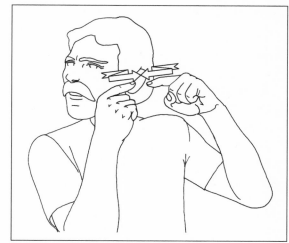

EAT

The flat "O" hand taps the mouth several times.

ELEPHANT

The "C" hand starts at the nose, then slides down in front of the body, representing an elephant's trunk.

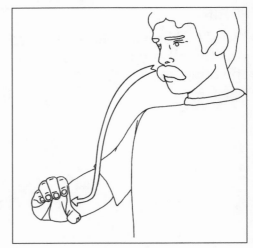

FALL DOWN

The base hand is held with palm facing up. The "inverted 2" hand moves from a "standing" position to a "lying" position, representing someone falling.

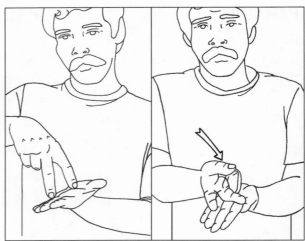

FATHER

The "5" hand is held up with the thumb tapping the forehead several times.

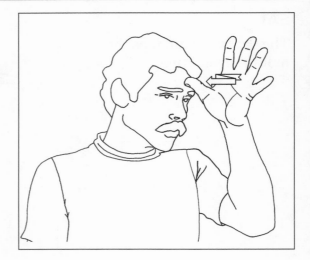

FINISHED

Both "5" hands are held palms up, then the palms flip down in a swift motion.

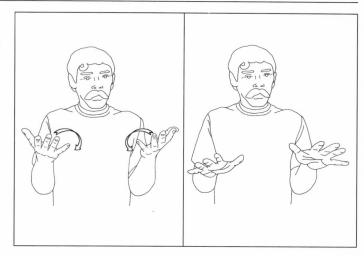

FIRE

Both "5" hands are held with the palms facing body, and fingers wiggle as the hands slowly rise.

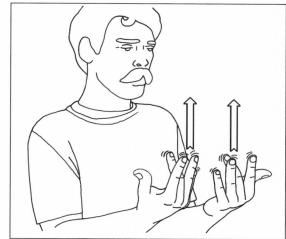

FISH

The flat base hand is held sideways with the fingertips touching the flat action hand at the wrist. The action hand moves forward, wiggling slightly, like a fish swimming.

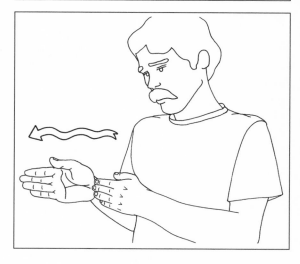

FLOWER

The flat "O" hand touches one side of the nose and then the other.

FLY

The base arm is held with the elbow bent. The claw action hand sweeps down to touch the base arm and closes into an "S" hand, as if catching a fly.

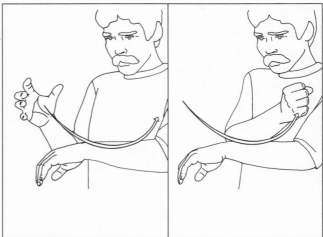

FROG

The "2" hand is held palm down under the chin, then the fingers bend and flick off of the thumb. The final position is shown with the fingers outstretched.

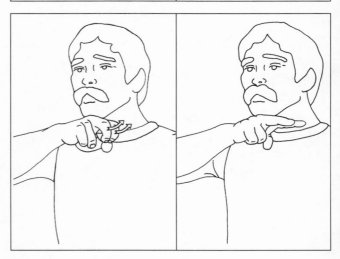

GET

The "5" hands are held palms facing inward, one hand above the other. Both hands close as they move towards the body.

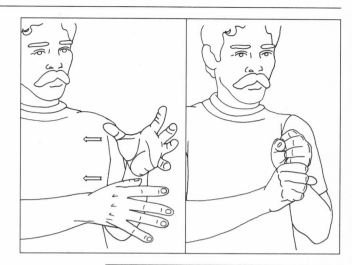

GIRL

The thumb draws a line from the jaw to the chin.

GO

Both "1" hands bend at the wrists and point in the direction one is going.

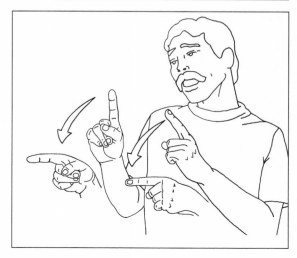

GOOD

The fingertips of
the flat hand
touch the lips,
then the hand
moves down
and away from
the body.

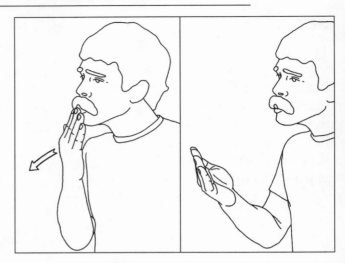

GRANDFATHER

The "5" hand is held
with the thumb to the
forehead, and then
moves down and away
from the face.

GRANDMOTHER

The "5" hand is held
with the thumb to the
chin, and then moves
down and away from
the body.

HAPPY

The flat hand pats the chest repeatedly with an upward movement, like the heart beating.

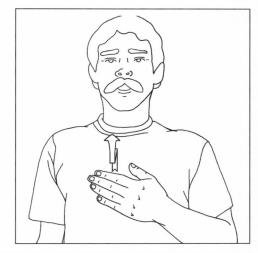

HEAD

The flat hand taps the side of the head.

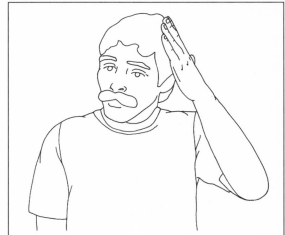

HEADACHE

Both "1" hands tap together several times in front of the forehead.

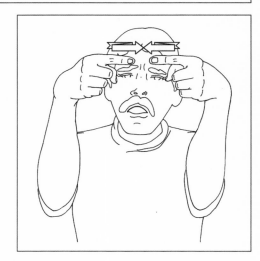

HELLO

The "5" hand waves back and forth.

HELP

The "S" hand is placed on top of the flat base hand, and both rise together in this position, as if the base hand is helping lift the fist.

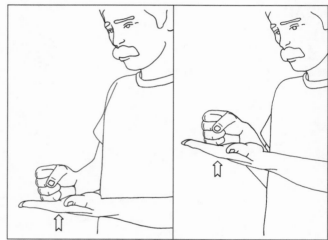

HIDE

With hunched shoulders, the cupped action hand is palm down over the base "A" hand to "hide" it, leaving only the thumb tip "peeking out."

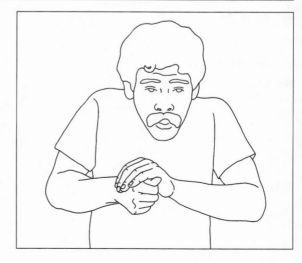

HOME

The flat "O" hand touches its fingertips to the chin and moves toward the ear.

HORSE

The closed "2"hand with the thumb extended touches the side of the forehead, with the fingers waving up and down.

HOT

The claw hand is held with the palm facing the mouth, then turned and dropped downwards, while mouthing "HHHH."

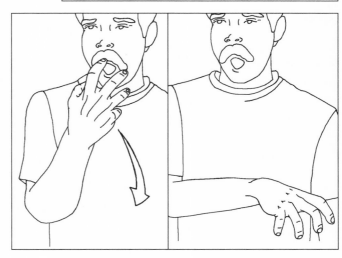

HOUSE

The fingertips of both flat hands join to make a roof angle. Then the flat hands separate with the palms facing, to represent the walls.

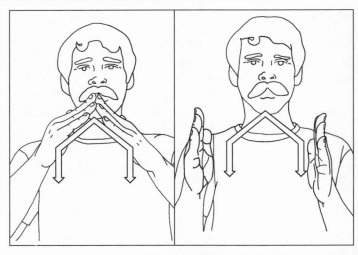

HUG

The hands grasp the upper arms, as if hugging yourself.

HURT

The index fingers of the "1" hands tap together several times.

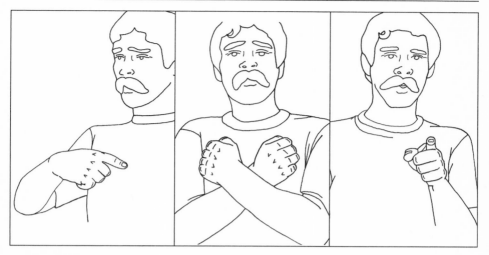

I LOVE YOU

The "1" hand points to yourself, indicating "I." The "A" hands cross over the chest, indicating "love." The "1" hand points, indicating "you."

I LOVE YOU

The "Y" hand is held up with the index finger extended.

ICE CREAM

The "S" hand moves up and down in front of the mouth, as if licking an ice cream cone.

IN

The flat "O" action hand is placed into the sideways "C" hand.

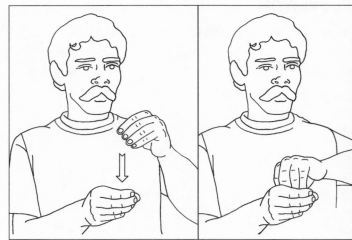

INSECT

The "3" hand is held with the thumb touching the nose. The two fingers wiggle together.

JUMP

The inverted "2" action hand rests on the palm of the base hand. The action hand springs up, as if jumping.

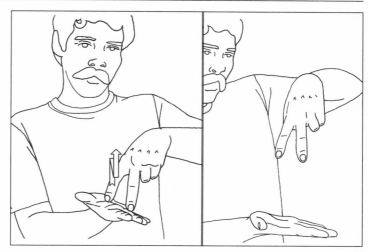

KETCHUP

The base "S" hand is held on its side. The "5" hand strikes the top of the base hand several times, as if striking the bottom of a ketchup bottle.

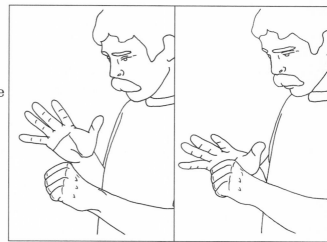

LION

The claw hand is raised to the opposite side of the head and arcs around the face, outlining a lion's mane.

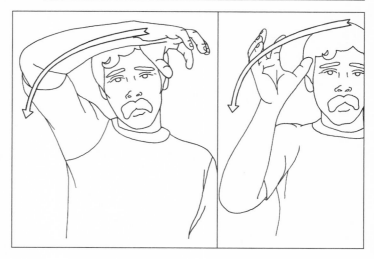

LITTLE

The two flat hands face each other, moving slightly in and out, to indicate a small size.

MEAT

The index finger and thumb grip the "5" hand near the last joint of the thumb, on the "meaty" part of the hand.

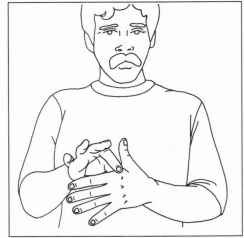

MILK

The claw hand, held on its side, squeezes into the "S" hand several times, as if milking a cow.

MINE

The flat hand touches the chest.

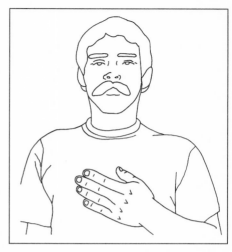

MONKEY

The hands scratch up and down at the sides, imitating a monkey.

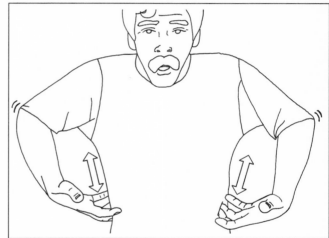

MOON

The hand is held up with the index finger and thumb forming a "C." The eyes look towards the hand, as if gazing up at the moon.

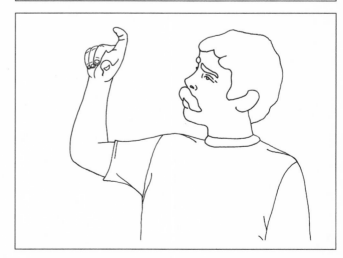

MORE

The two "flat O" hands tap
their fingertips together
several times.

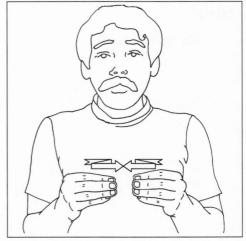

MOSQUITO

The "9" action
hand touches
the base forearm,
then takes a "5"
shape and slaps
the forearm, as if
slapping a
mosquito.

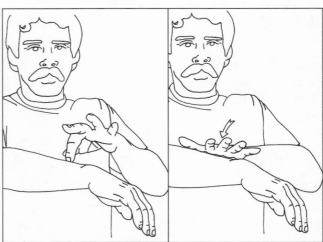

MOTHER

The thumb of the "5" hand
taps the chin several times.

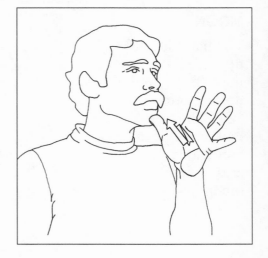

MOUSE

The "1" hand is held up with the finger brushing across the nose.

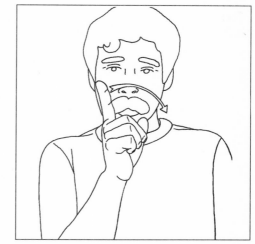

NO

The first two fingers close down to touch the extended thumb several times.

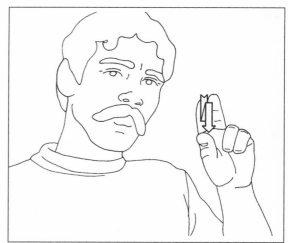

ORANGE

The claw hand closes several times, as if squeezing an orange.

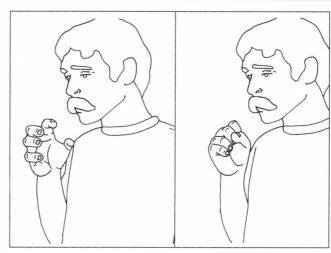

OUT

The fingertips of the "flat O" action hand are inserted in the sideways "C" hand. The action hand is pulled out.

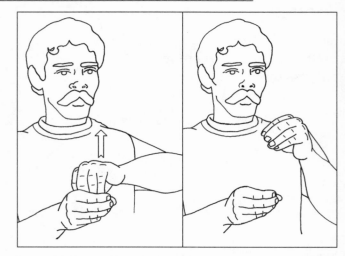

OVER

The flat base hand is held palm down while the flat action hand, with the palm facing the body, arcs over the base hand.

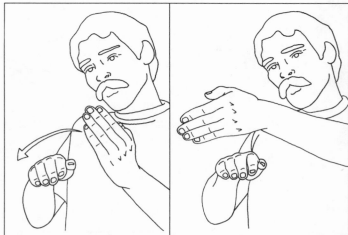

PAIN

The index fingers of the "1" hand tap together several times at the location of the pain.

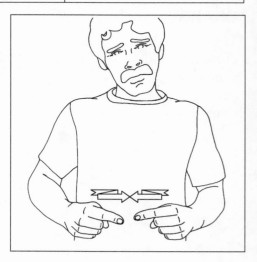

PIE

The flat base hand is held with the palm up. The flat action hand makes two slicing motions, as if slicing a pie.

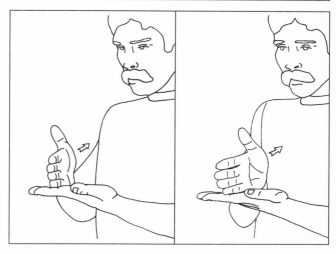

PLAY

The "Y" hands are held at the sides and pivot back and forth at the wrists.

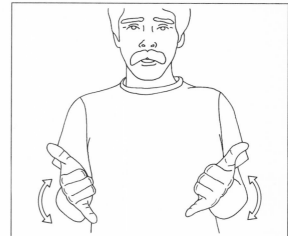

PLEASE

The flat hand touches the chest and moves in a circular motion.

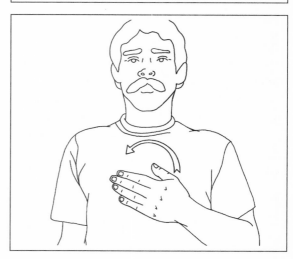

POPCORN

The modified "X" hands alternately "pop" into the "1" hand position.

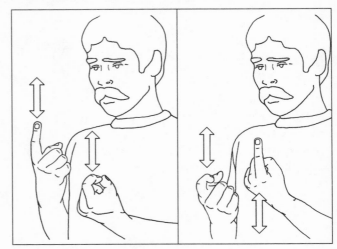

POTATO

The base "S" hand is horizontal and the bent "2" action hand taps the back of the base hand several times, like a hoe digging a potato.

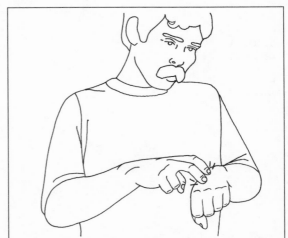

RABBIT

The first two fingers are held up with palms facing behind you and the fingers quiver like rabbit ears.

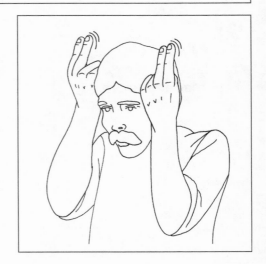

RAIN

The "5" hands are held at head level with the palms down. The hands drop down at a slight angle, like rain falling in the wind.

RUN

Both "L" hands are in front of the chest with the index finger of the rear hand linking to the thumb of the forward hand. Both hands move toward the body and the forward index finger bends.

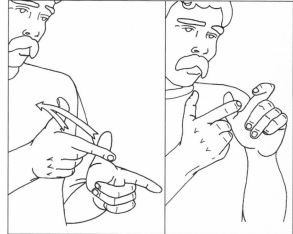

SAXOPHONE

Both hands are in the claw position, with the fingers moving, and the cheeks puffed, as if playing a saxophone. Any instrument can be mimed.

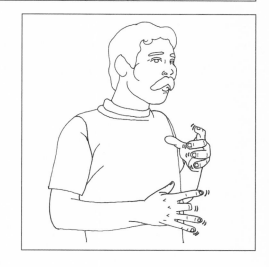

SCARED

Both "S" hands
are held with the
palms facing
each other. Then
suddenly, as they
move toward
each other, they
open to "5"
hands with the
fingers shaking.

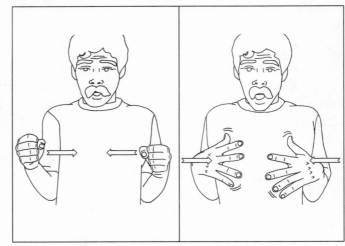

SEARCH

The "C" hand
passes in
front of the
face in circu-
lar motions.

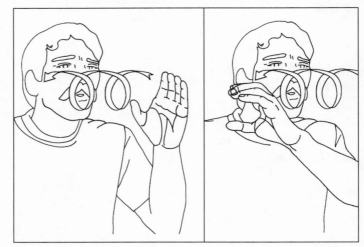

SHARE

The flat base hand is vertical
with the thumb extended
upward. The flat action hand
is also vertical and slides
back and forth across the
index finger of the base hand.

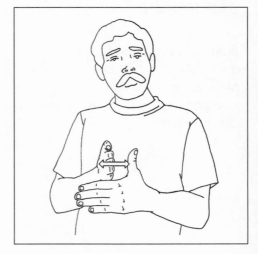

SHOES

The two sideways "S" hands tap together several times.

SICK

One "8" hand touches the forehead and the other "8" hand touches the stomach.

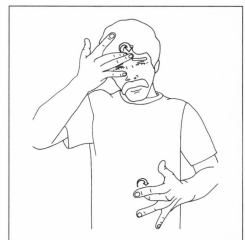

SISTER

The "L" hand thumb touches the chin and then moves down to meet the lower "L" hand.

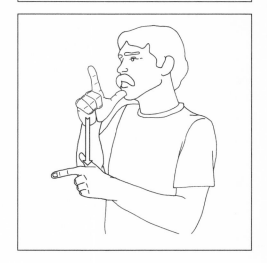

SIT

The first two fingers of one hand "sit" on the other two fingers.

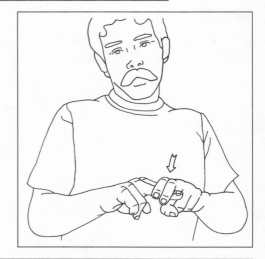

SLEEP

The "5" hand is held in front of the face and the eyes shut as the fingers close into a "flat O" at the chin.

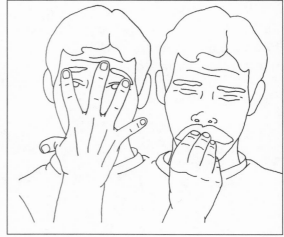

SNAKE

The bent "2" hand moves forward in small arching motions.

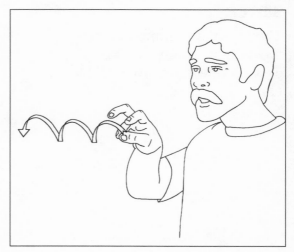

SNOW

The "5" hands come down slowly with the fingers wiggling.

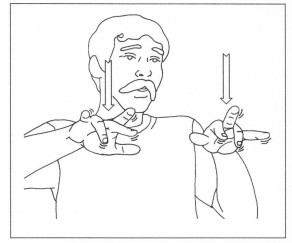

SOCKS

Both "1" hands are pointing down, one higher than the other. The fingers move up and down, brushing each other as they pass.

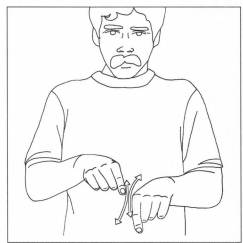

SORE THROAT

The "1" hands tap fingertips together several times at the throat.

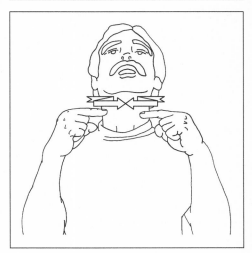

SORRY

The "S" hand moves in a circular motion on the chest.

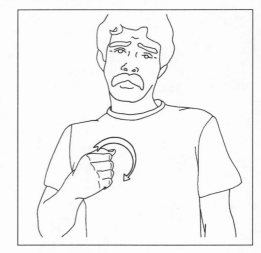

SPIDER

Both claw hands face down, with the little fingers interlocked. The hands slowly move forward with the fingers wiggling like legs.

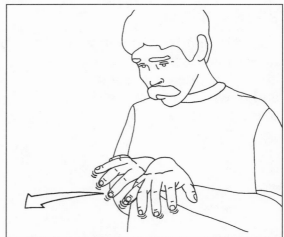

SPOON

The first two fingers sweep down to the cupped base hand and up to the mouth, as if using a spoon.

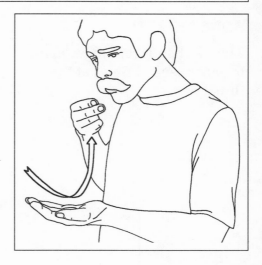

SQUIRREL

The bent "2" hands tap together several times at the fingertips.

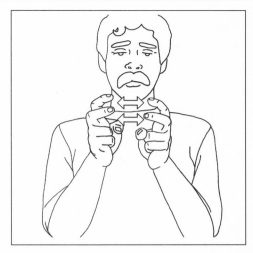

STOMACH ACHE

The index fingers tap together several times at the stomach.

STOP

The flat base hand is held palm up and the flat action hand comes down on its side, striking the base palm.

SUN

The "C" hand is held up, and the eyes look up at the hand.

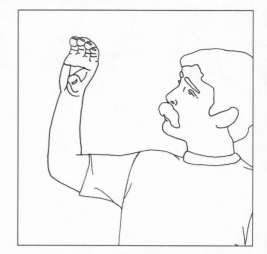

TELL

The "1" hand touches the lips and moves out toward the person being addressed.

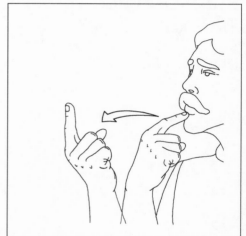

THANK YOU

The fingertips of the flat hand touch the lips and the hand falls forward, toward the person being thanked.

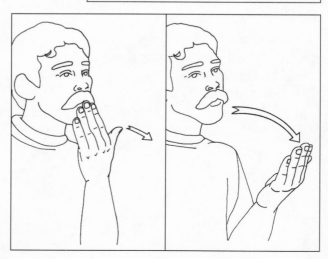

THROW

The "flat O" hand is raised and drawn toward the body then quickly moves forward and opens into a "5" hand.

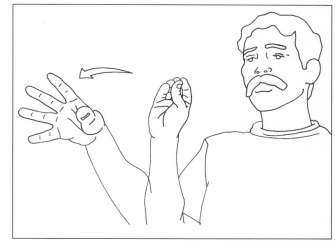

THUNDER

The index finger points to the ear, and then both "S" hands are held at chest level and move alternately in and out.

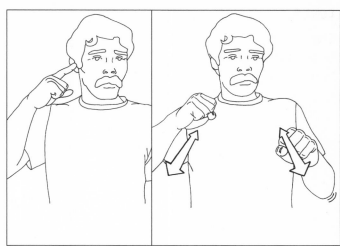

TICKLE

The "1" hand wiggles at the side, as if tickling.

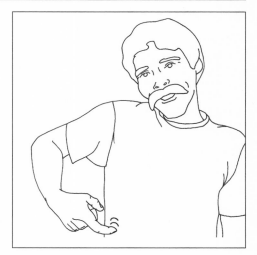

TIRED

Both cupped hands are held with the palms facing the body, fingertips touching the chest. The hands pivot down.

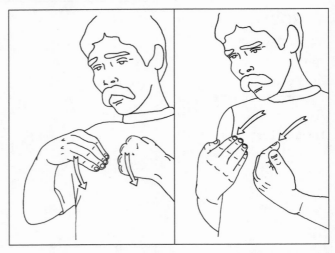

TOILET

The "T" hand shakes slightly back and forth.

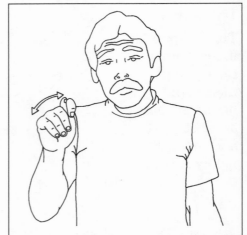

TOUCH

The "8" hand taps the back of the flat base hand one or two times.

TURTLE

The cupped hand is held over the top of the "A" hand, representing a turtle in its shell. The thumb of the "A" hand wiggles to show turtle's head moving.

UNDER

The cupped base hand is held palm down. The flat action hand moves down underneath the base hand.

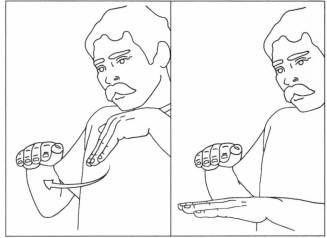

UP

The "1" hand points upward several times.

WAIT

Both "5" hands are held to one side with palms up, and the fingers wiggle.

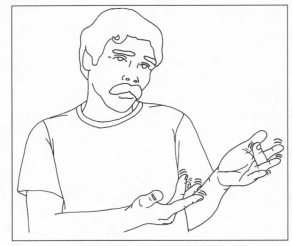

WANT

Both flat hands are held with palms facing up, then hands form claw shapes as they move in slightly toward the body.

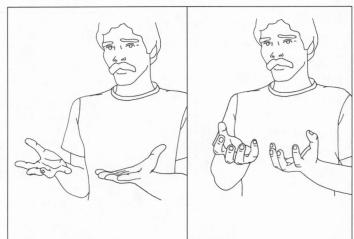

WARM

The "A" hand is held in front of the mouth with the fingers falling forward one at a time, from the index finger to the little finger.

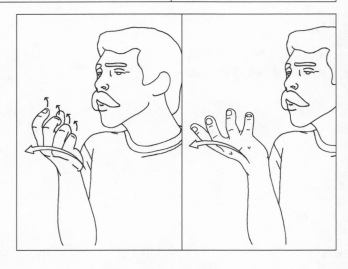

WATER

The index finger of the "6" hand taps the side of the mouth twice.

WHERE

The "1" hand waves from side to side, pivoting at the wrist.

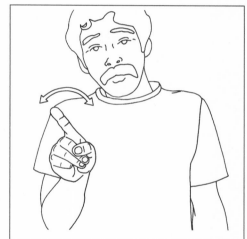

WORK

One "S" hand taps the top of the other "S" hand several times at the wrist.

WORM

The palm of the flat base hand faces to the side. The index finger of the action hand is placed in the palm. The index finger curls and straightens as it moves across the palm like a worm crawling.

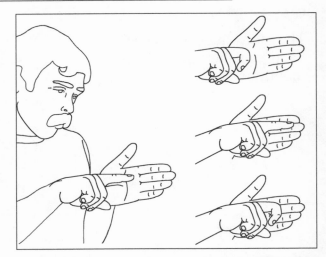

YES

The "S" hand moves up and down at the wrist, like a head nodding.

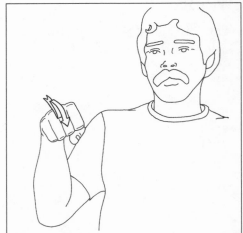

YOU'RE WELCOME

The flat open hand moves gracefully from in front of the face to the waist.

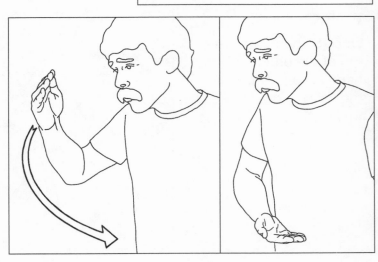

Notes

REFERENCES

BLAKESLEE, THOMAS. *The Right Brain: A New Understanding of the Unconscious Mind and its Creative Powers.* Garden City: Anchor Press/Doubleday, 1980.

BOLINGER, DWIGHT. *Aspects of Language.* New York: Harcourt Brace Jovanovich, 1975.

BROWN, ROGER. *A First Language: The Early Stages.* Cambridge: Harvard University Press, 1973.

BRUNER, JEROME. *Child's Talk: Learning to Use Language.* New York: W. W. Norton and Company, 1983.

BRYANT, PETER. *Perception and Understanding in Young Children: An Experimental Approach.* New York: Basic Books, 1974.

BULLOWA, MARGARET, ed. *Before Speech: The Beginning of Interpersonal Communication.* New York: Cambridge University Press, 1979.

FIELD, TIFFANY M. and TEDRA A. WALDEN. "Production and Perception of Facial Expressions in Infancy and Early Childhood." *Advances in Child Development and Behavior* 16 (1982): 171-211.

LIEBERMAN, PHILIP. *The Biology and Evolution of Language.* Cambridge: Harvard University Press, 1984.

MOORE, TIMOTHY E., ed. *Cognitive Development and the Acquisition of Language.* New York: Academic Press, 1973.

NELSON, KATHERINE. *Event Knowledge: Structure and Function in Development.* Hillsdale: Lawrence Erlbaum Associates, 1986.

_____. *Making Sense: The Acquisition of Shared Meaning.* New York: Academic Press, 1985.

WIEMAN, JOHN M. and RANDALL P. HARRISON, eds. *Nonverbal Interaction* Beverly Hills: Sage Publications, 1983.

INDEX

ORDER FORM

Telephone orders Call toll free: 1 (800) 566-6656. Have your Visa, MasterCard, or American Express number and expiration date ready.
Fax orders (206) 452-1340. For other information call (206) 452-1917.

Postal orders Checks require 10 working days to clear; postal or bank money orders are processed immediately.

Please send _____ copy(ies) of Toddler Talk.

1 Book	$12.95 ea.
1 Video	$10.00 ea.
Shipping	$ 3.00
Total	$_____
Tax	$_____(7.8% or current rate for Washington State only)
Total	$_____

5-10 copies: 20% discount; 5 or more copies: shipping paid C.O.D.

10 or more copies: Contact Stratton-Kehl for quantity discount.

Send payment to: **Stratton-Kehl Publications, Inc.**

P.O. Box 28567
Bellingham, WA
98228-0567

Payment

__ Check

__ Money Order

__ Credit Card: ___ Visa   ___ MasterCard   ___ Am Exp

Card Number:_____

Name on Card:_____Exp. Date:___/___

Customer Information (please print)

Name: _____

Address: _____

City/State/Zip: _____

Phone: _____

ORDER FORM

Telephone orders Call toll free: 1 (800) 566-6656. Have your Visa, MasterCard, or American Express number and expiration date ready.
Fax orders (206) 452-1340. For other information call (206) 452-1917.

Postal orders Checks require 10 working days to clear; postal or bank money orders are processed immediately.

Please send _____ copy(ies) of Toddler Talk.

1 Book	$12.95 ea.
1 Video	$10.00 ea.
Shipping	$ 3.00
Total	$_____
Tax	$_____ (7.8% or current rate for Washington State only)
Total	$_____

5-10 copies: 20% discount; 5 or more copies: shipping paid C.O.D.

10 or more copies: Contact Stratton-Kehl for quantity discount.

Send payment to: **Stratton-Kehl Publications, Inc**.

P.O. Box 28567
Bellingham, WA
98228-0567

Payment

__ Check

__ Money Order

__ Credit Card: ___ Visa   ___ MasterCard   ___ Am Exp

Card Number:_____

Name on Card:_____Exp. Date:___/___

Customer Information (please print)

Name: _____

Address: _____

City/State/Zip: _____

Phone: _____